THE NBA FINALS

by Drew Silverman

Published by ABDO Publishing Company, PO Box 398166, Minneapolis, MN 55439. Copyright © 2013 by Abdo Consulting Group, Inc. International copyrights reserved in all countries. No part of this book may be reproduced in any form without written permission from the publisher. SportsZone™ is a trademark and logo of ABDO Publishing Company.

Printed in the United States of America,
North Mankato, Minnesota
112012
012013

Editor: Chrös McDougall
Series Designer: Craig Hinton

Photo Credits: Ken Levine/Getty Images, cover; Winslow Townson/AP Images, title; John Biever/ Sports Illustrated/Getty Images, 5, 59 (bottom, left); Elaine Thompson/AP Images, 9; Jack Smith/ AP Images, 11; NBA Photos/NBAE/Getty Images, 13; John Rooney/AP Images, 16; AP Images, 19, 25, 29, 35, 58 (top, left and right), 59 (top); Gene Herrick/AP Images, 21; Dan Farrell/NY Daily News Archive/Getty Images, 31; Dick Raphael/Sports Illustrated/Getty Images, 37; Manny Millan/Sports Illustrated/Getty Image, 39; Carl Skalak/Sports Illustrated/Getty Images, 43, 58 (bottom); Reed Saxon/AP Images, 45; Elisa Amendola/AP Images, 47; Mark Lennihan/AP Images, 49, 59 (bottom, right); Michael Conroy/AP Images, 51; Lynne Sladky/AP Images, 57; Cal Sport Media/AP Images, 60 (top); Doug Pizac/AP Images, 60 (bottom, left); Mark Phillips/AP Images, 60 (bottom, right)

Cataloging-in-Publication Data
Silverman, Drew.
 The NBA Finals / Drew Silverman.
   p. cm. -- (Sports' great championships)
Includes bibliographical references and index.
ISBN 978-1-61783-671-8
1. Basketball--Tournaments--United States--Juvenile literature. 2. National Basketball Association--History--Juvenile literature. I. Title.
796.323/64--dc22

                                                        2012946164

Jean M. Thomsen Memorial Library
P.O. Box 99 / 105 N. Gershwin St.
Stetsonville, WI 54480
715-678-2892

TABLE OF CONTENTS

The Running of the Bulls

I t was Game 6 of the 1998 National Basketball Association (NBA) Finals. The Utah Jazz led the Chicago Bulls 86–85 as the clock ticked down— eight seconds, seven seconds. It was Michael Jordan's time to take over.

The Bulls' guard had the ball just beyond the free-throw line. In a split-second, he crossed over the dribble to his left hand. Then he elevated in front of Jazz defender Byron Russell. Jordan held his follow-through as he watched his shot. It hit nothing but net. With 5.2 seconds remaining in the game, the Bulls led 87–86.

Michael Jordan hits the game-winning shot against the Utah Jazz in Game 6 of the 1998 NBA Finals. The shot clinched the Chicago Bulls' sixth title in eight years.

The Jazz missed a three-pointer. The clock expired after that. That night in 1998, Jordan and the Bulls capped off an amazing run of six NBA championships in eight seasons. Among those wins were some of the most extraordinary and famous moments in NBA Finals history. And in those NBA Finals, Jordan cemented himself as one of sport's greatest and most popular players ever.

A Dynasty Is Born

Jordan quickly proved he was a great player in the NBA. He came into the league in 1984 and won his first Most Valuable Player (MVP) Award in 1988. The 6-foot-6 guard was extremely talented on both offense and defense. He could take over games single-handedly.

What made Jordan a legendary player, however, was his performance and killer instinct on the biggest stage: the NBA Finals.

The Bulls had long been a team on the rise behind Jordan. In 1989 and 1990, they reached the Eastern Conference Finals. Finally, in 1991, they broke through to the NBA Finals. It was a classic test of greatness. On one side was rising star Jordan and the unproven Bulls. On the other side was superstar guard Earvin "Magic" Johnson and the Los Angeles Lakers. The Lakers had captivated the nation in reaching eight of the 11 previous NBA Finals, winning five of them.

Not Half Bad

Michael Jordan was at his best in Game 1 of the 1992 NBA Finals against the Portland Trail Blazers. He scored 35 points—in the first half. Jordan hit six three-pointers during that time. The Bulls' star only scored four points in the second half. Still, his team cruised to a 122–89 victory.

Jordan was not fazed. He averaged 31.2 points per game as the Bulls dispatched the old guard four games to one in the seven-game series. He added 11.4 assists, 6.6 rebounds, 2.8 steals, and 1.4 blocks per game. The Lakers dynasty of the 1980s was finished. The Bulls' dynasty had begun.

"I'm not even thinking about [winning] any other championships right now," Jordan said during the Bulls' first championship celebration. "I just want to enjoy this one for as long as I can."

Of course his attention soon turned toward winning another NBA title. And that is what he did. Jordan led the Bulls past the Portland Trail Blazers in 1992 and the Phoenix Suns in the 1993. Jordan claimed the NBA Finals MVP Award in all three victories. The new NBA dynasty in Chicago appeared unstoppable. Or was it?

John on the Spot

Victory in the 1993 NBA Finals was on the line. But the hero for the Chicago Bulls was not Michael Jordan or Scottie Pippen. It was point guard John Paxson. The Bulls trailed the Phoenix Suns 98–96 in Game 6. Less than 10 seconds remained.

Jordan passed the ball to Pippen, who drove to the basket. Pippen then dished the ball to forward-center Horace Grant. Grant then moved it to a wide-open Paxson. Paxson was standing behind the three-point line. He drained the go-ahead shot with 3.9 seconds left.

Then Grant blocked the final shot attempt by Phoenix. The Bulls had clinched their third straight championship. "I couldn't think of a more dramatic finish," Bulls coach Phil Jackson said. "I've never seen a Finals game end like this in my years in the NBA."

Round 2

Jordan was easily the best player in the world. The Bulls were an unstoppable force. Then on October 6, 1993, at the peak of his career, Jordan decided to retire and pursue a professional baseball career instead.

Small forward Scottie Pippen kept the Bulls in the playoffs. But the Houston Rockets had no problem stepping into the top spot. They won the NBA title in 1994 and 1995. Jordan was not yet finished, though.

He rejoined the Bulls in the spring of 1995. Before the 1995–96 season, the team added power forward Dennis Rodman as well. The Bulls became an absolute force. They won an NBA-record 72

regular-season games. Then they dispatched of the Seattle SuperSonics in six games in the NBA Finals. A new dynasty had begun.

Stopping the Jazz

If there was one team that could have stopped the Jordan-led Bulls in the 1990s, it might have been the Utah Jazz. Utah point guard John Stockton was one of the NBA's best. He combined with MVP power forward Karl Malone to form one of the NBA's all-time best duos. Unfortunately for Jazz fans, however, Jordan saved some of his most extraordinary NBA Finals performances for games against Utah.

Jordan clinched Game 1 of the 1997 NBA Finals over Utah with a buzzer-beating jump shot. Then, with the series tied, Jordan came into Game 5 suffering from the stomach flu. The man nicknamed "Air Jordan" battled exhaustion and dehydration throughout the game. But he still played 44 minutes and finished his legendary effort with 38 points. That included a three-pointer in the final minute as the Bulls won 90–88.

Two nights later in Game 6, Jordan got the ball with 26 seconds left and the game tied at 86–86. Naturally, the Jazz quickly double-teamed him. But Jordan was more than just a scorer. The double team left sharpshooting reserve guard Steve Kerr open about 15 feet from the basket. So Jordan passed and Kerr hit the go-ahead shot. A dunk a few seconds later by Bulls forward Toni Kukoc sealed the 90–86 win and another NBA title for Chicago.

The Bulls and Jazz appeared to be even more evenly matched when they met in the 1998 NBA Finals. Each had 62–20 records in the regular season. Jordan and Malone were number one and two in MVP voting. Then they split the first two games in the Finals. But in Game 3, Chicago downed Utah 96–54 in the biggest blowout in NBA Finals history. Another win in Game 4 had the Bulls on their way. Only a heroic 39-point performance by Malone kept the Jazz alive for Game 6.

Michael Jordan holds the NBA Finals MVP trophy while coach Phil Jackson holds the NBA championship trophy after the Chicago Bulls' victory in the 1998 NBA Finals.

The series went back to Utah. That is when Jordan truly took over. In what proved to be his final game for Chicago, Jordan scored on a driving layup, made a key steal against Malone, and then drained the title-winning jump shot—all in the last minute. Of all the great players who shined in the NBA Finals over the years, Jordan showed in that minute why many consider him to be the best.

The Early Years

Basketball began in 1891 at a gymnasium in Springfield, Massachusetts. The game known as "basket ball" developed into modern basketball over the next several decades. The game on a professional level, however, took a while to take hold.

Various professional leagues came and went from 1898 until 1946. That is when the Basketball Association of America (BAA) was founded. The league was not very popular or stable early on. Some teams existed

Joe Fulks, one of the best players of his day, led his Philadelphia Warriors to what is considered the first NBA Finals championship in 1947.

only so arena owners could make more money while the more popular hockey teams were on the road.

Nonetheless, the BAA held its first championship in 1947. Star forward Joe Fulks led the Philadelphia Warriors to the title. He scored 37 points in Game 1 and 34 points in the clinching Game 5 against the Chicago Stags. Those numbers were huge in a league where the average for an entire team was just 67.8 points per game.

On August 3, 1949, the BAA and the National Basketball League merged to become the NBA. That 1947 series is now considered to be the first NBA Finals. Fulks and his 1947 Philadelphia Warriors are considered to be the first NBA champions.

The First NBA Dynasty

Professional basketball in the late 1940s was much different than it is today. The 1947–48 BAA season only had eight teams. As of 2012 there were 30 in the NBA. Few players at the time stood taller than 6-foot-6. Now even many NBA guards are at least that tall. On the court, there was no shot clock yet. That led to very slow, low-scoring games. There was also no three-point line.

As such, some considered basketball to be boring. The league had trouble getting fans excited about professional basketball. That began to change in 1948–49. The Minneapolis Lakers brought in center George

A Tiny Bonus

Each player on the Philadelphia Warriors received a $2,000 bonus for winning the 1947 BAA title. In 1952, the Minneapolis Lakers split $7,500 as a prize. That was considered a good bonus at the time. However, it hardly compares to today's NBA salaries. In 2011, the Dallas Mavericks got to split $2 million after winning the NBA title.

Mikan and rookie forward-center Jim Pollard that season. The team added rookie forward-center Vern Mikkelsen and rookie guard Slater Martin one year later. Mikan and Pollard led the Lakers to the 1949 BAA title. Then the Hall of Fame foursome led the Lakers to NBA titles in 1950, 1952, 1953, and 1954. The NBA had its first dynasty.

All four players were stars. However, Mikan was in a class of his own. The Illinois native stood 6 feet, 10 inches tall. That made him a giant among men in those years. Most of Mikan's Lakers teammates were only a few inches taller than 6 feet.

Mikan played like a giant, too. He was tremendously strong and skilled around the basket. In the 1949 BAA Finals, Mikan broke his wrist. He had to play the last two games against the Washington Capitols with a cast. Yet he still scored 22 points in Game 5 and 29 points in the series-clinching Game 6 win.

Minneapolis Lakers teammates tease star center George Mikan (99) after a game against the New York Knicks in 1949.

"He wore a cast that was as hard as a brick," said Washington forward-center Horace "Bones" McKinney, who guarded Mikan in the NBA Finals, "… and it didn't bother his shooting a bit."

Mikan averaged 32.2 points per game in the 1950 NBA Finals against the Syracuse Nationals. But he was not the Game 1 hero. That honor belonged to rookie Bob Harrison. He made a 40-foot jump shot at the buzzer to win the game. However, the Lakers closed out the series when Mikan scored 40 points in a Game 6 win.

The Lakers might have recorded the NBA's first three-peat in 1951 had Mikan not suffered a slight fracture in his ankle late in the season. He tried to play through pain in the playoffs. But the Rochester Royals stopped the Lakers in the Western Conference Finals. The Royals went on to beat the New York Knicks in a thrilling seven-game NBA Finals.

Mikan was healthy again the next season, though. And he was once again a force for the Lakers in the NBA Finals. The Knicks put up a strong fight. The series went all the way to seven games. Mikan struggled a bit early. But he scored 26 points and grabbed 17 rebounds in a Game 3 win.

New York, New York

From 1949 to 1954, the only NBA Finals to not include the Minneapolis Lakers was in 1951. However, it might have been the most significant for the NBA. The 1951 series was played between the Rochester Royals and the New York Knicks. The contest between the two teams from New York state generated great interest in the league on the East Coast.

The series proved to be entertaining. It was the first NBA Finals to go the full seven games. Plus, through 2012, it was the only time in NBA Finals history that a team (the Knicks) lost the first three games and then won the next three to force a Game 7.

Perhaps most importantly, the series involved a New York City team. That meant the big city's newspapers covered the NBA Finals much more completely than in years past. However, basketball still did not replace baseball on the front pages of the newspapers.

Then he had 32 points in a Game 5 win. Finally the Lakers closed out the series when Mikan scored 22 and had 19 rebounds in Game 7. The 8,600 fans at the Minneapolis Auditorium stormed the court in celebration.

The 1953 NBA Finals was a rematch between the Lakers and the Knicks. This time, the Lakers lost the first game at home. Then they swept the next four games, including three on the road, to win the title.

"The New York newspapers were all saying that the series wouldn't go back to Minneapolis," Mikan said. "They were right. It didn't."

In 1953–54, Mikan was 29 and battling through several injuries. His historic career would soon be over. But he played all 72 games that season. Then he led the Lakers to another title. The NBA Finals against the Nationals went to seven games. Syracuse's Hall of Fame forward-center

Coach 'Em Up

John Kundla of the Minneapolis Lakers became the first NBA coach to win multiple league titles. He won five total championships with the Lakers between 1949 and 1954. Only two coaches, Phil Jackson (11 titles) and Red Auerbach (9 titles), had exceeded Kundla through 2012.

Minneapolis Lakers center George Mikan secures a rebound during a 1954 game against the New York Knicks.

Dolph Schayes limited Mikan to just 11 points. But Pollard added 21 to help Minneapolis win 87–80.

Mikan retired after that, having led Minneapolis to five championships in his six seasons. He had a brief and forgettable comeback in 1955–56. However, his play from 1948–49 to 1953–54 made him one of the most dominant players in NBA history.

"He literally carried the league," fellow Hall of Famer Bob Cousy said. "He gave us recognition and acceptance when we were at the bottom of the totem pole in professional sports."

The Celtics Dynasty

T he Minneapolis Lakers became the NBA's first true dynasty. But after George Mikan retired, attendance at Lakers home games dipped to below 3,000 fans per contest. So in 1960 they moved to Los Angeles and became the NBA's first West Coast team.

That made the NBA a truly national league for the first time. However, the league still had only nine or fewer teams until the 1966–67 season. The NBA might as well have only had one team during that era, though.

Center Bill Russell (6) led the Boston Celtics to 11 championships between 1957 and 1969. No US professional sports team has ever matched that level of success.

Red and Russell

Between 1957 and 1969, the Boston Celtics won an unprecedented 11 NBA championships in 13 seasons. They made the NBA Finals in all but one of those years. Several Hall of Fame players played a role in that era. Among them were guards Bob Cousy and Bill Sharman and swingmen John Havlicek and Sam Jones. Coach Red Auerbach was the Celtics' coach when they won their first nine NBA titles from 1957 to 1966. But only one player had a role in each of the Celtics' 11 NBA Finals victories. Bill Russell was at the center—literally—of all those teams.

Russell was not a flashy player. His longtime rival Wilt Chamberlain was known as the NBA's greatest scorer of the era. Russell was also a good scorer. And nobody could match the 6-foot-9 California native on defense. He dominated under the basket grabbing rebounds and blocking shots.

That low-post presence showed from the beginning. The Celtics reached the NBA Finals in Russell's rookie season of 1956–57. NBA MVP Cousy led the way that season. But Russell passed a big test in the NBA Finals. St. Louis Hawks power forward Bob Pettit kept his team alive for seven games against the heavily favored Celtics. Boston won only when Pettit's last-second tap-in rolled around the rim and dropped out at the buzzer of double overtime in Game 7.

"The first one is always the hardest," Auerbach said. "And it's also the most satisfying."

Sweet Six

Until Michael Jordan arrived, the debate about the NBA's best player of all time centered around Bill Russell. The Boston Celtics' center revolutionized defense during an offensive period. Russell, a five-time NBA MVP, led the league in rebounds per game five times. Blocked shots were not recorded at the time. As evidenced by his record 11 NBA titles, Russell was often at his best in the playoffs. In 1960, he set an NBA Finals record with 40 rebounds in Game 2 against the St. Louis Hawks. Russell did not have the huge scoring numbers that his rival Wilt Chamberlain did. But he certainly had Chamberlain beat when it came to championships.

"There are two types of superstars," Celtics teammate Don Nelson said. "One makes himself look good at the expense of the other guys on the floor. But there's another type who makes the players around him look better than they are, and that's the type Russell was."

Eight Straight

Pettit and Russell had some great battles during the late 1950s. They actually almost played for the same team. In 1956, the Hawks drafted Russell and immediately traded him to Boston. It seemed like a good move at the time. St. Louis got future Hall of Famers Ed Macauley and Cliff Hagan in return.

That trade helped the Hawks reach the NBA Finals four times in five years from 1957 to 1961. However, they lost to the Celtics in three of those series. The Hawks' only win came in 1958. That year Pettit scored 50 points in Game 6 to clinch the title.

The Los Angeles Lakers then replaced St. Louis as the Western Division power. Los Angeles was another team with its share of talent. The Celtics had swept the Minneapolis Lakers in 1959. But behind future Hall of Famers power forward Elgin Baylor and shooting guard Jerry West, the Lakers reached the NBA Finals seven times between 1962 and 1970.

Over that period, home attendance at Lakers games rose from just more than 6,000 per game to more than 13,000 per game. Fans were unable to witness a championship during that era, however. Those mostly belonged to the Celtics. Beginning in 1962, Boston beat the Lakers in six of the next eight NBA Finals.

Wilt Chamberlain of the Philadelphia Warriors posts up against Bill Russell of the Boston Celtics during a 1962 game.

Boston needed overtime of a seventh game to squeak out a victory over the Lakers in the 1962 NBA Finals. The up-and-coming Lakers appeared ready to end Boston's winning streak at four going into the 1963 NBA Finals. But rookie Havlicek joined seven other future Hall of Famers to hold off Los Angeles in six games.

Another NBA superstar stepped up to try to stop Russell and the Celtics in 1964. The NBA Finals that year featured the first championship-round contest between Russell and Chamberlain. Chamberlain, a San Francisco Warriors center, was 7-foot-1 and 275 pounds. That gave him two inches and 60 pounds over Russell.

The 1964 Finals went much the way most of their rivalry did, though. Chamberlain was stellar. He scored at least 30 points in three of the five games. He added at least 20 rebounds in every game. But the Celtics proved to be the superior team. Russell had the key dunk in the final seconds of Game 5 to give Boston its sixth straight title.

"The thrill never goes from winning," Auerbach said. "But maybe the reasons change. First, it was just trying to win a title. Now it is a question of going down as the greatest team of all time."

Boston met Los Angeles in the NBA Finals in 1965 and 1966. Baylor was injured for the Lakers in 1965. Los Angeles managed just one win in the first NBA Finals to average more than 10,000 fans per game. The Celtics won the other four by an average margin of 21 points.

The Lakers made it closer in the 1966 NBA Finals. The series went all the way to Game 7. But in that game, Russell scored 25 points and got 32 rebounds. The Celtics' 95–93 win gave Auerbach one more championship in his final season. It was Boston's eighth consecutive championship. No NBA team—and no team in any major professional US sport—has matched that feat. Many believe no team ever will.

The Celtics' Revival

Auerbach had retired after the 1966 season. The Celtics remained an NBA power under Russell, who was now a player-coach. But in 1967, nobody was going to beat the Philadelphia 76ers.

Chamberlain was traded to the 76ers during the 1964–65 season. In 1966–67, the growing NBA added a tenth team and expanded the playoffs to eight teams from six. No matter, the 76ers averaged 125.2 points per game while winning an amazing 68 games. They were so good that Chamberlain was able to step back his offense and focus on other areas of his game. The Celtics still won 60 games that season. They had

New Team, Same Story

When the Philadelphia 76ers won the NBA championship in 1967, Alex Hannum became the first head coach to win the NBA Finals with two different teams. He had also guided the St. Louis Hawks to the NBA championship in 1958. Since Hannum, only two other head coaches had led multiple teams to an NBA title through 2012. Hannum said his 1967 76ers team was the best. "That was the greatest team in the history of basketball," Hannum said. "I'm talking about all kinds of basketball, including the Dream Teams."

only surpassed that once during their run of eight titles. Yet in the Eastern Division Finals, the 76ers blew by the Celtics in five games. Chamberlain soon got his first NBA title with a win over the Warriors.

"Everyone who knows the game of basketball knows who really is the greatest," 76ers guard Wali Jones said of Chamberlain after the win.

Russell and the Celtics were not done quite yet, though. The Celtics overcame Chamberlain and the 76ers in the 1968 playoffs. Then they beat the Lakers in six games to win a tenth championship.

The Celtics' last hurrah came, fittingly, against the Lakers. Russell and Sam Jones were each 35 years old by the time the 1969 NBA Finals started. And Los Angeles had a new weapon that season: Chamberlain.

A New Award

In 1969, the NBA Finals MVP Award was given out for the first time. The first winner was Los Angeles Lakers guard Jerry West. He took home the honor in 1969 even though the Lakers lost that series to the Boston Celtics. Through 2012, that remained the only time the NBA Finals MVP has played for the losing team. Beginning in 2009, the award was renamed the Bill Russell NBA Finals MVP Award in honor of the 11-time NBA champion.

John Havlicek of the Boston Celtics goes up for a basket during the 1968 NBA Finals against the Los Angeles Lakers. Boston won to claim its tenth championship.

The Finals proved to be a battle featuring two key player matchups. Russell and Chamberlain battled it out on the post. Havlicek and West faced off on the perimeter. The Lakers had the advantage early on, taking Games 1 and 2. Then Havlicek and Russell led Boston to wins in Games 3 and 4. The teams traded wins after that, leading to Game 7. It was the third NBA Finals Game 7 between these teams in the decade. Boston ended up winning all three.

In his final NBA game, Russell had six points and 21 rebounds. He retired later that summer, as did Jones. And just like that, the Celtics dynasty—at least this edition of it—was over.

A Growing League

The New York Knicks won what might have been the decade's most memorable championship right away in 1970. It was also the first NBA Finals to be entirely broadcast live on television. Game 3 featured one of the most amazing shots in NBA history. Los Angeles Lakers guard Jerry West heaved the ball 60 feet to tie the game at the fourth-quarter buzzer. Despite the miracle shot, the Knicks ultimately won in overtime to take a 2–1 series lead.

Willis Reed of the New York Knicks, *front*, and Wilt Chamberlain of the Los Angeles Lakers, *back*, battled in a memorable 1970 NBA Finals.

The MVP Triple Crown

In 1969–70, Willis Reed of the New York Knicks did something historic. He became the first player in NBA history to win the All-Star Game MVP, the regular-season MVP, and the NBA Finals MVP in the same season. Since then, only Chicago Bulls star Michael Jordan (1996 and 1998) and Los Angeles Lakers center Shaquille O'Neal (2000) had captured the MVP triple crown in the same season through 2012.

The Lakers evened the series in Game 4. Then the Knicks were dealt a blow in Game 5. Center Willis Reed tripped over the Lakers' Wilt Chamberlain in the first quarter. Reed, the league's MVP that season, tore a leg muscle and had to leave the game. The Knicks were down 25–15 at the time. But without Reed, they changed to a small lineup. New York went on to win that fifth game 107–100.

In Game 6, Chamberlain had 45 points and 27 rebounds. The Lakers won, and the series shifted back to New York for Game 7. Reed was not expected to play. However, he received some last-minute injections in his injured leg. That allowed him to hobble out onto the court to a rousing ovation from the New York fans.

"The scene is indelibly etched in my mind," said Knicks point guard Walt Frazier, who had 36 points and 19 assists in Game 7. "Because if that did not happen, I know we would not have won the game."

Reed could barely move, but he managed to make the first two baskets for the Knicks. He also played tough defense on the much bigger Chamberlain. The inspired Knicks led 69–42 at halftime. In front of 19,500 fans, they went on to win 113–99.

Parity Takes Over

The Knicks' win signaled the beginning of the NBA's first era of parity. Through the Boston Celtics' 1969 NBA championship, two teams had won a combined 16 of the first 23 BAA/NBA Finals. But the league was rapidly growing.

A Golden Upset

The 1975 championship series produced one of the biggest upsets in the history of the NBA Finals. Many experts had predicted that the Golden State Warriors would miss the playoffs. They indeed made the playoffs with a 48–34 record. But the Washington Bullets had won a league-best 60 games. Then the Warriors struggled in winning the Western Conference Finals while the Bullets cruised in the East. Furthermore, the Warriors had lost nine of their previous 12 matchups against the Bullets. That dated back a couple of seasons.

In the Finals, though, Golden State left no doubt as to which was the better team. The Warriors swept the Bullets in four straight games.

"It has to be the greatest upset in the history of the NBA Finals," said Rick Barry, who took home MVP honors after averaging 29.5 points in the series for Golden State.

Between 1960 and 1974, the NBA expanded from eight to 18 teams. In fact, professional basketball was growing enough that a rival league formed in 1967–68. The American Basketball Association (ABA) introduced new concepts in an effort to take attention from the NBA. Perhaps the most noteworthy addition was the three-point line. The ABA ultimately folded. But four former ABA teams joined the NBA in 1976–77 to create a 22-team league.

The larger league made it harder for one team to dominate. During the 10 seasons from 1969–70 to 1978–79, eight different teams won the NBA Finals. The Milwaukee Bucks were one of those teams. They had only been founded in 1968–69. But in 1971 they featured future Hall of Fame point guard Oscar Robertson and Hall of Fame center Lew Alcindor (later known as Kareem Abdul-Jabbar). The Bucks swept the new Baltimore Bullets in four games to win an NBA title in only their third year.

The Lakers stepped up next. They had been one of the NBA's best teams in the 1960s behind stars such as Chamberlain and West. However, Los Angeles had lost the first seven NBA Finals it reached after moving from Minneapolis in 1960. Including the Minneapolis Lakers' 1959 NBA Finals appearance, the Lakers had lost eight in a row.

That finally changed in 1972 against the Knicks. For West, it was the only championship of his 14-year career. For Chamberlain, it was his

Milwaukee Bucks center Kareem Abdul-Jabbar hits the winning hook shot over Boston Celtics defenders during Game 6 of the 1974 NBA Finals.

second NBA title. West did not play his best in the five-game series, but Chamberlain picked up the slack. He capped the series with 24 points and 29 rebounds in Game 5. "I played terrible basketball in the Finals and we won," West later said, ". . . but maybe that's what a team is all about."

The Lakers and Knicks met in an NBA Finals rematch in 1973. This time, New York won in five games. Reed was named NBA Finals MVP for the second time.

Boston came back in the picture after that. Celtics center Dave Cowens was the Game 7 hero in 1974. That afternoon, Cowens outscored

Milwaukee's Abdul-Jabbar 28–26 in the decisive game. Two years later, the Celtics engaged in a hard-fought NBA Finals series with the Phoenix Suns. Boston won Game 6 to clinch the series. However, it was Game 5—a triple-overtime thriller—that many basketball fans still talk about.

"That was the most exciting basketball game I've ever seen," said Rick Barry, who worked the event as part of the broadcasting team. "They just had one great play after another."

One of those great plays was a 15-foot jumper by Boston's John Havlicek in the final seconds of the second overtime. However, Phoenix's Gar Heard then hit a 25-foot jumper at the buzzer to force a third overtime. Celtics reserve Glenn McDonald was the hero in the third

Two-Man Show

NBA Finals MVP Dennis Johnson and fellow guard Gus Williams led the 1978–79 Seattle SuperSonics. Combined, the two players scored more than half of Seattle's points in the NBA Finals that year. Johnson had 113 points in the five-game series victory over the Washington Bullets. Williams had 145 points. That made a two-man total of 258 points. Every other SuperSonics player combined scored just 247 points.

THE NBA FINALS

The Boston Celtics' John Havlicek hits his famous double-overtime shot against the Phoenix Suns in Game 5 of the 1976 NBA Finals. Boston won in triple overtime.

overtime. He scored six points to help Boston to a 128–126 victory. Two days later, the 1976 championship belonged to the Celtics.

The Celtics, Knicks, and 1978 Washington Bullets (the Bullets moved from Baltimore in 1973) kept the NBA title on the East Coast five times during the 1970s. The decade was proof that the NBA's western expansion was working. The Golden State Warriors—based in Oakland, California— won the NBA title in 1975. Two years later, the Portland Trail Blazers won their first championship. And then in 1979, the Seattle SuperSonics closed out the decade with another NBA title for a West Coast team. Soon, one particular West Coast team and one specific East Coast team dominated the league for a decade.

The Rivalry Resumes

T he NBA had steadily grown since the 1947 BAA Finals. Few would argue that it had ever been more popular or more exciting than it was in the 1980s. Two new superstars joined the NBA's two traditional powers in 1979–80. During the 1980s, either Earvin "Magic" Johnson and his Los Angeles Lakers or Larry Bird and his Boston Celtics played in every NBA Finals. And in three of those NBA Finals, both rivals faced off against each other for the title.

Earvin "Magic" Johnson smiles while holding the trophy after leading his Los Angeles Lakers to the 1980 NBA championship.

Fans relished in the Johnson-Bird rivalry even before they reached the NBA. In 1979, the two superstars met in the college basketball national championship game. Johnson's Michigan State Spartans beat Bird's Indiana State Sycamores in what *Washington Post* columnist Michael Wilbon described as the game that "launched the popularity of college basketball and began the Golden Age of professional basketball." Approximately 20 million people watched on television.

That excitement carried over to the NBA. The league had grown greatly in popularity since the Celtics and Minneapolis Lakers first met in the 1959 NBA Finals. However, some felt the league had grown stale during the late 1970s. Johnson, the flashy, always-smiling point guard, brought new life to the NBA's glamour team. Those teams became known as the "Showtime" Lakers. The stoic, multi-talented forward Bird, meanwhile, proved the perfect foil for the blue-collar Celtics.

Magic Show

Johnson had a superstar teammate waiting for him when he arrived in Los Angeles. Lakers center Kareem Abdul-Jabbar would eventually retire as the NBA's all-time leading scorer. However, it was a game without Abdul-Jabbar in which the rookie Johnson first lived up to his "Magic" nickname.

The Lakers met the Philadelphia 76ers in the 1980 NBA Finals. Los Angeles took a 3–2 series lead. However, Abdul-Jabbar sprained his ankle. In his absence, Johnson had one of the remarkable performances in NBA Finals history. That night, the 6-foot-9 point guard played all five positions during the course of the game. That included time filling in at center for the 7-foot-2 Abdul-Jabbar. Johnson finished Game 6 with 42 points, 15 rebounds and seven assists. That clinched the title for the Lakers.

"It was amazing, just amazing," said 76ers star Julius Erving.

The stage was set for a decade of incredible growth and popularity in the NBA. In 1981, Bird and the Celtics beat the Houston Rockets in six games to win the title. Then the Lakers and 76ers squared off in back-to-back NBA Finals. Johnson and the Lakers won in 1982. Then Erving and bruising center Moses Malone led the 76ers to a four-game sweep

He Said It

"We're so competitive anyway that there was a dislike there. I even hated him more because I knew he could beat me."—Los Angeles Lakers guard Magic Johnson on his rivalry with Boston Celtics forward Larry Bird in 1983. Finally, in 1984, fans got the marquee matchup they had been waiting for.

Lakers-Celtics

The Lakers and Celtics had not faced off for a championship since 1969. Bird and Johnson had not faced off for a championship since college in 1979. Both finally happened again in 1984.

The series lived up to its billing. Johnson and Bird both seemed to play better with championships on the line—and against each other. Johnson set an NBA Finals record with 21 assists in Game 3. Then Bird came back with 29 points and 21 rebounds in Game 4. The series featured two overtime games. It fittingly came down to a decisive Game 7.

The Lakers needed a police escort to safely get to the Boston Garden for the game. When they got there, Bird led his Celtics to victory. Bird scored 20 points and added 12 rebounds in the 111–102 win. He was named NBA Finals MVP with averages of 27.4 points, 14 rebounds, and 3.2 assists. Johnson averaged 18 points and dished out an NBA Finals-record 95 assists.

Fans only had to wait one season for a rematch. This time Boston cruised to an easy 148–114 win in Game 1. But the Lakers stormed back to win four of the next five games to capture the title. Abdul-Jabbar averaged 26 points per game in the series. The 38-year-old earned

NBA Finals MVP honors. For the Celtics, Bird was hampered by injuries to his elbow, back, and finger. The Boston star made just 12 of 29 shots in the decisive Game 6.

Bird matched Johnson by winning his third NBA title in 1986. He won Finals MVP honors in leading his team to victory over the Rockets. So when Bird and Johnson met for their third and final NBA Finals showdown in 1987, bragging rights were on the line.

Abdul-Jabbar was 40 years old by then. But the Celtics' frontcourt was not in great shape, either. Boston power forward Kevin McHale played with a broken foot. Center Robert Parish dealt with a severely sprained ankle. After three games, the Lakers led 2–1. The next game proved to be the turning point in the series.

With 12 seconds left in Game 4, Bird drilled a three-point shot to put Boston ahead 106–104. Abdul-Jabbar cut the lead to one on a free throw. Then the Lakers got the ball back when McHale knocked it out of bounds. After a timeout, Johnson got the ball. He drove across the lane and lifted a hook shot while being guarded by three future Hall of Famers—Bird, McHale, and Parish. The shot hit nothing but net. Bird then missed a potential game-winning shot at the buzzer.

"You expect to lose on a sky hook," Bird said, referring to Abdul-Jabbar's signature shot. "You don't expect it to be from Magic."

Five for Five

The Los Angeles Lakers won five championships during the 1980s. Only three players were members of all five teams, though. They were All-Star point guard Earvin "Magic" Johnson, guard Michael Cooper, and superstar center Kareem Abdul-Jabbar.

Five days later, the Lakers were NBA champions. Johnson had 16 points and 19 assists in the series-clinching Game 6. Abdul-Jabbar scored 32 points. The Celtics' run of titles was over. But the Lakers' dynasty of the 1980s was not done yet.

The Bad Boys

A new power was emerging in the Eastern Conference. The Detroit Pistons featured the talented backcourt of Isiah Thomas and Joe Dumars. They also featured two physical post players in center Bill Laimbeer and forward Rick Mahorn. The aggressive Pistons eliminated Boston in the

All Things Must End

The 1989 Finals brought an end to Kareem Abdul-Jabbar's legendary career. The Lakers' 42-year-old center had announced his retirement before the NBA Finals against the Detroit Pistons. He exited late in Game 4 to a rousing ovation from the Los Angeles crowd. He scored just seven points in the game.

Abdul-Jabbar finished his 20-year career with six NBA championships. One came with the Milwaukee Bucks and the other five with the Lakers. He was named NBA Finals MVP for the Bucks in 1971 and for the Lakers in 1985. He also retired as the NBA's all-time leading scorer, a record he still held in 2012.

"Kareem was probably, with his size and his sky hook, the most dominating force in our league as far as getting a basket any time you want it," Boston Celtics star Larry Bird said.

1988 playoffs. Then the "Bad Boys" Pistons came within one win of beating the Lakers in the NBA Finals.

The veteran Lakers won dramatic contests in Games 6 and 7. Lakers power forward James Worthy had the only triple-double of his 12-year career in Game 7. That earned him MVP honors. The Lakers became the first team to repeat as champions since the Celtics in 1968 and 1969.

The Lakers' quest for three in a row came to an abrupt end in 1989, though. The Pistons defeated the Lakers in a four-game sweep in 1989. Then they beat the Portland Trail Blazers in five games in 1990.

Detroit Pistons forward Dennis Rodman lifts teammate Isiah Thomas into the air after the Pistons won a second consecutive NBA title in 1990.

Soon, however, those three 1980s dynasties were replaced by a new one—led by one player in particular.

6 ★ Chapter ★

A New Era

T he 1990s were all about Michael Jordan, Scottie Pippen, and the Chicago Bulls. They wrapped up their second NBA Finals three-peat in 1998. That gave the Bulls six NBA championships in eight seasons. The Houston Rockets claimed the two titles in between.

After that, two big men nicknamed "The Twin Towers" took over. Veteran center David Robinson and young forward Tim Duncan led the Spurs to their first NBA Finals in 1999. The opposing New York Knicks

The San Antonio Spurs' David Robinson, *left,* holds the NBA championship trophy while Tim Duncan holds the NBA Finals MVP trophy after winning the 1999 title.

hardly had a chance with future Hall of Fame center Patrick Ewing sidelined with a foot injury.

Duncan averaged 27.4 points and 14 rebounds in the five-game series. Robinson chipped in 16.6 points and 11.8 rebounds. In Game 4, the Spurs' Twin Towers outrebounded the Knicks by themselves, 35–34. Robinson retired in 2003. Behind Duncan, though, the Spurs remained an NBA force into the next decade.

Lakers' Revival

Another NBA force emerged soon after. The Los Angeles Lakers, now featuring guard Kobe Bryant and center Shaquille O'Neal, won all three NBA titles from 2000 to 2002.

O'Neal was a mammoth force under the basket. He was often compared to the Lakers' original star center George Mikan, who was so dominant the NBA had to change its rules to slow him down. O'Neal's dominance showed against the Indiana Pacers in the 2000 NBA Finals. He averaged 38 points and 16.7 rebounds in the six-game victory. That included three games in which he scored at least 40 points.

Star guard Allen Iverson and the 76ers upset the Lakers in Game 1 of the 2001 NBA Finals. But O'Neal, Bryant, and the Lakers rallied to win the next four games and a second consecutive championship. Los Angeles made it a three-peat in 2002 by defeating the New Jersey Nets in a

four-game sweep. That marked the third championship for O'Neal and Bryant. It was the ninth for Lakers coach Phil Jackson. He had also guided Jordan and the Bulls to six titles during the 1990s.

Duncan, Robinson, and the Spurs stepped in to prevent the Lakers from making it four in a row. San Antonio beat the Lakers in the second round of the playoffs. Then the Spurs won a second NBA title in a six-game victory over the Nets.

The loss sent a message to the Lakers that they could be beaten. So they responded by adding more future Hall of Famers in point guard Gary

Big Shot Bob

Robert Horry is considered to be one of the greatest role players in NBA history. Horry was a forward with a nice outside touch and a knack for making big shots. He won seven NBA championships with three different teams. He was on the Houston Rockets' title-winning teams in 1994 and 1995. He then won three straight championships with the Los Angeles Lakers from 2000 to 2002. Finally, Horry added titles with the San Antonio Spurs in 2005 and 2007.

Payton and power forward Karl Malone in 2003–04. The star-studded squad indeed returned to the NBA Finals that year. However, the starless Detroit Pistons upset them four games to one. The Lakers' big-name players could not overcome Detroit's strong teamwork and defense. And before the next season, only Bryant remained of the big-name stars in Los Angeles.

Those Steady Spurs

Basketball had become accustomed to flashy superstars leading their teams to titles. First it was Earvin "Magic" Johnson and the Lakers. Then came Jordan and the Bulls. And Bryant, O'Neal, and the Lakers stepped in after that.

The Spurs and the Pistons were hardly flashy. San Antonio had an elite player in Duncan. But his nickname was "The Big Fundamental"—not quite "Magic" Johnson or "Air" Jordan. The Pistons had five starters who played strong defense and worked hard. That approach worked for those teams. Detroit and San Antonio met for the championship in 2005. After seven games, the Spurs proved to be the best. Duncan totaled 25 points and 11 rebounds in Game 7 en route to earning series MVP honors.

"He put his team on his shoulders and carried them to a championship," Pistons center Ben Wallace said. "That's what the great players do."

Tim Time

Tim Duncan had one of the best performances of his career in Game 6 of the 2003 NBA Finals. That night, the San Antonio Spurs overcame a nine-point deficit in the fourth quarter to win the championship. Duncan torched the New Jersey Nets for 21 points, 20 rebounds, 10 assists, and eight blocks. He came two blocks away from recording the first quadruple-double in NBA postseason history.

The Heat Is On

The 2006 NBA Finals featured a little bit of everything—a historic comeback, a spectacular individual performance, and the return of two legends of the game.

The Miami Heat became just the third team in NBA history to win the NBA Finals after losing the first two games. Miami's star guard Dwyane Wade put on a scoring exhibition. He averaged 34.7 points in the series. In Games 3, 4, and 5, he averaged 40.3 points in three Miami wins. And then he scored 36 in Game 6 as Miami clinched its first championship.

The series also marked a return to the top for two basketball icons. The Heat had traded for center Shaquille O'Neal two years earlier. He won his fourth NBA title in 2006. And Miami coach Pat Riley—a four-time champion with the Lakers in the 1980s—took over early in the season and led the Heat to the 2006 title.

In 2007, Duncan and the Spurs made their fourth NBA Finals appearance in nine years. And once again, Duncan and the Spurs prevailed over a flashier team. This time it was rising superstar LeBron James and the Cleveland Cavaliers. James was on his way to being recognized as one of the most talented players ever. The experience edge in this series, however, was obvious.

Duncan and Spurs coach Gregg Popovich each won their fourth championship. But it was Tony Parker who proved to be the difference for San Antonio. The French point guard averaged 24.5 points in the series as the Spurs won all four games.

Contrast in Styles

The 2009 NBA Finals proved to be a classic matchup of small vs. big. It featured one of the league's best guards (the Los Angeles Lakers' Kobe Bryant) against one of the league's best big men (Dwight Howard of the Orlando Magic). Howard averaged 15.4 points, 15.2 rebounds, and 4 blocks in the series. But Bryant averaged 32.4 points and 7.4 assists as the Lakers won the championship in five games.

They're Back!

The Lakers and the Celtics each had rebuilding periods after their successful 1980s. The Lakers were once again the class of the NBA in the early 2000s behind Bryant and O'Neal. With Bryant still around, and upon adding All-Star forward Pau Gasol, the Lakers were back among the best going into the 2007–08 season. As it turned out, so were the Celtics. Before the season, Boston added bruising forward Kevin Garnett and sharpshooter Ray Allen to a squad that already included forward Paul Pierce. The result was the return of the NBA's biggest rivalry.

Including the Minneapolis Lakers era, the Celtics and Lakers had met 10 times in the NBA Finals. They met for an eleventh time in 2008. Pierce averaged 21.8 points as the Celtics won the series in six games. But Bryant and the Lakers got revenge two years later. He averaged 28.6 points in the seven-game Lakers victory.

The faces had changed over the decades, but the Celtics-Lakers rivalry remained must-see in the NBA. However, in 12 meetings through 2012, Boston held the advantage with nine victories.

Next Generation

The Lakers and Celtics were strong teams, but they could no longer dominate. In 2010–11, the Miami Heat were the talk of the NBA. Before that season, the Heat had re-signed star guard Dwyane Wade and also signed free agents Chris Bosh and James.

"Not two, not three, not four, not five, not six, not seven," James said, in reference to how many championships the trio would win in Miami.

They had to wait for their first, though. In 2011, a Dallas Mavericks squad composed mostly of veterans searching for their first championship met Miami in the NBA Finals. James, Wade, and Bosh fueled a Heat team that was younger, quicker, and stronger. But in the end, the experienced Mavericks won the series in six games.

Another team emerged in 2012 to challenge the Heat. Just four years earlier, the Oklahoma City Thunder had been the Seattle SuperSonics. The team won a miserable 20 games in its final season in Seattle. But in 2007

NBA superstars LeBron James (6) of the Miami Heat and Kevin Durant (35) of the Oklahoma City Thunder face off in the NBA Finals in 2012.

it had drafted a young forward named Kevin Durant. Over the next few years the team added other young players through the draft as well.

By 2012, the small-city Thunder had emerged as the biggest threat to the big-city Heat. The two teams met in a much-anticipated NBA Finals. This time, however, the Heat proved unstoppable. Oklahoma City opened with a 105–94 win in Game 1. Then James, Wade, Bosh, and the Heat took the next four. The final game was not close as Miami won 121–106.

The 2012 NBA Finals were not as close as many hoped. But they highlighted a bright future for the league. With new stars emerging and more teams winning championships, the NBA Finals appears to be headed into a new generation of greatness.

TIMELINE

Joe Fulks and the Philadelphia Warriors defeat the Chicago Stags in five games to win the first BAA championship on April 22.
1947

Center George Mikan leads the Minneapolis Lakers to their first NBA championship. They win four more titles through 1954.
1949

The Boston Celtics win the NBA title by defeating the St. Louis Hawks. This begins a stretch of 11 championships in 13 years.
1957

Forward Bob Pettit scores 50 points in Game 6 as the Hawks defeat the Celtics to win the NBA Finals.
1958

Philadelphia 76ers center Wilt Chamberlain leads his team to an NBA title with a six-game win over the San Francisco Warriors.
1967

Bird and Johnson meet in the NBA Finals for the first time. Bird's Celtics defeat Johnson's Lakers in seven games.
1984

Bird and Johnson play against each other in the NBA Finals for the third and final time. The Lakers defeat the Celtics in six games.
1987

Michael Jordan plays in the NBA Finals for the first time and leads his Chicago Bulls past the Lakers for the title.
1991

The Bulls complete their first of two three-peats during the 1990s when they defeat the Suns in six games.
1993

Playing with a severe case of the flu, Jordan scores 38 points in 44 minutes to lead the Bulls past the Utah Jazz in Game 5 of the NBA Finals.
1997

Despite a torn muscle in his leg, Knicks center Willis Reed plays Game 7 of the NBA Finals as the Knicks beat the Lakers.

1970

Kareem Abdul-Jabbar wins his first of six NBA titles, this time with the Milwaukee Bucks. He is named NBA Finals MVP.

1971

In an all-time classic game, the Celtics defeat the Phoenix Suns 128–126 in triple overtime in Game 5 of the NBA Finals.

1976

Earvin "Magic" Johnson replaces the injured Abdul-Jabbar and leads the Lakers over the 76ers in Game 6 of the NBA Finals.

1980

Larry Bird leads the Celtics to their fourteenth NBA title with a victory over the Houston Rockets.

1981

Jordan wins his sixth and final NBA title. He clinches the title by making a jump shot with 5.2 seconds left in Game 6 against the Jazz.

1998

Shaquille O'Neal and Kobe Bryant lead the Lakers to their third straight title with a sweep over the New Jersey Nets.

2002

Tim Duncan wins his fourth NBA title when his San Antonio Spurs beat the Cleveland Cavaliers, four games to none.

2007

For the first time in more than two decades, the Celtics and Lakers meet in the NBA Finals. Boston wins in six games.

2008

The Dallas Mavericks complete an upset of the Miami Heat to win the NBA title. The Heat come back to win the 2012 title.

2011

CHAMPIONSHIP OVERVIEW

The Trophy

The Larry O'Brien NBA Championship Trophy is awarded to the team that wins the NBA Finals at the conclusion of each basketball season. The award is named after Larry O'Brien, who

served as commissioner of the NBA between 1975 and 1983. The trophy is recreated each year for permanent possession of the winning team.

The Legends

Kareem Abdul-Jabbar (Milwaukee Bucks and Los Angeles Lakers): Six titles, two NBA Finals MVPs from 1971 to 1988

Kobe Bryant (Lakers): Five titles, two NBA Finals MVPs since 2000

Earvin "Magic" Johnson (Lakers): Five titles, three NBA Finals MVPs from 1980 to 1988.

Michael Jordan (Chicago Bulls): Six titles, six NBA Finals MVPs from 1991 to 1998

Bill Russell (Boston Celtics): 11 titles from 1957 to 1969

The Victors

Boston Celtics: 17 NBA titles since 1957

Minneapolis/Los Angeles Lakers: 16 NBA titles since 1949

Chicago Bulls: Six NBA titles since 1991

San Antonio Spurs: Four NBA titles since 1999

GLOSSARY

assist
> A pass that directly leads to a teammate's made basket.

dynasty
> A team that wins several championships over a short period of time.

free agent
> A professional athlete who is allowed to sign a contract with any team.

icons
> Revered players viewed as symbols of a team, league, or sport.

rebound
> The gathering of a missed shot after it hits the rim or the backboard.

retire
> To officially end one's career.

rival
> An opposing person or team that brings out particular emotion from a player, a team, or its fans.

rookie
> A first-year player in the NBA.

FOR MORE INFORMATION

Selected Bibliography

Fox, Larry. *The Illustrated History of Basketball*. New York: Grosset & Dunlap, 1974.

Great Athletes: Basketball. Hackensack, NJ: Salem Press, 2010.

The Official NBA Encyclopedia. New York: Doubleday, 2000.

Total Basketball: The Ultimate Basketball Encyclopedia. Wilmington, Delaware: Sport Media Publishing, 2003.

Wright, Frank L. *The Ultimate Basketball Book*. Crystal Bay, Nevada: Sierra Vista Publications, 2007.

Further Readings

Grange, Michael. *Basketball's Greatest Stars*. Richmond Hill, Ontario: Firefly Books, 2010.

Reynolds, Bill. *Rise of a Dynasty : The '57 Celtics, the first banner, and the dawning of a new America*. New York: New American Library, 2010.

The Macrophenomenal Pro Basketball Almanac. New York: FreeDarko High Council, 2008.

The Undisputed Guide to Pro Basketball History. New York: FreeDarko High Council, 2010.

Web Links

To learn more about the NBA Finals, visit ABDO Publishing Company online at **www.abdopublishing.com**. Web sites about the NBA Finals are featured on our Book Links page. These links are routinely monitored and updated to provide the most current information available.

Places to Visit

Naismith Memorial Basketball Hall of Fame
1000 West Columbus Avenue
Springfield, MA 01105
(413) 781-6500
www.hoophall.com
This hall of fame and museum highlights the greatest players and moments in the history of basketball. Among the people enshrined here are Michael Jordan, George Mikan, and Bill Russell.

The Sports Museum
100 Legends Way
Boston, MA 02114
(617) 624-1234
www.sportsmuseum.org
Located at the TD Garden, home of the Boston Celtics, the museum celebrates Boston sports, including the Celtics' record 17 NBA Finals wins.

INDEX

About the Author

Drew Silverman is a sportswriter based in Philadelphia. The Syracuse University grad was a writer and editor at ESPN before returning to Philly, where he served as the sports editor for *The Bulletin* newspaper. He is now a content manager at Comcast SportsNet.

HANUKKAH,
OH HANUKKAH

Susan L. Roth

Dial Books for Young Readers  New York

Hanukkah, oh Hanukkah,

come light the menorah.

Let's have a party,
we'll all dance the hora.

Gather round the table,

we'll give you a treat.

Dreidels to play with,

latkes to eat.

And while we are playing,

the candles are burning low.

One for each night,
they shed a sweet light,

to remind us of days long ago.

One for each night,
they shed a sweet light,

to remind us of days long ago.

HANUKKAH, OH HANUKKAH

Ha - nu - kkah, oh Ha - nu - kkah, come light the me - no - rah.

Let's have a par - ty, we'll all dance the ho - ra.

Gath - er round the ta - ble, we'll give you a treat.

Drei - dels to play with, lat - kes to eat.

To Rebecca Roth's great-grandchildren, in order of appearance:

Liat, Shira, Paul, Sophia, Lena, Max, Molly, Danielle, and **Rebecca,**

and all the others yet to come.

✱

Thank you to the third-grade students at Beth Tfiloh School in Baltimore, Maryland.
Many thanks also to Rona Zuckerberg, Shelly Malinow, Shoshana Krupp,
Shirley Avin, Carolyn Van Newkirk, and Zipora Schorr.
Thank you for the papers: Nobuko and Masato Kasuga, Michael Laufer, and
Jill Tarlau. And thank you to Olga R. Guartan.

✱

Published by Dial Books for Young Readers
A division of Penguin Young Readers Group
345 Hudson Street, New York, New York 10014
Copyright © 2004 by Susan L. Roth
All rights reserved
Manufactured in China on acid-free paper
Designed by Teresa Kietlinski
Text set in Pabst
1 3 5 7 9 10 8 6 4 2

Library of Congress Cataloging-in-Publication Data
Roth, Susan L.
Hanukkah, oh Hanukkah / Susan L. Roth.
p. cm.
Summary: A family of mice celebrates the eight days of Hanukkah
with friends in this illustrated version of the holiday song.
ISBN 0-8037-2843-3
1. Children's songs—Texts. [1. Hanukkah—Songs and music. 2. Songs.] I. Title.
PZ8.3.R747Han 2004   782.42164'0268—dc22   2003013165

To make these collages, I used paste, tweezers, scissors, lace,
and papers from every basket in my studio.